FEAST

poems by Kala Joy

Pure Joy Press
158 Harmony Hill Lane
Waynesville, NC 28786
kalaalak@gmail.com
kalajoy.net
Michelle Neve c. 2013

"Eden is here and the world is new.
We'll eat whatever we want to."

(Wendy Rule, "Lilith," *Guided by Venus)*

with eternal gratitude to my Beloved Shiva
who has helped me to live and breathe and grow
and to all who have held me in their hearts with love
throughout my healing
adventure

A New Season

I do not wish for death
that falling back from the light of afternoon
into skull white settling into dark earth.
Not the grand final end of these fingers,
this skin over bones, this wide eyed
face still astonished when summer green
floods the landscape, hides the mountain
range, localizes vision to the edges,
thickens the waist of the wild lands.

No, but a death still of sorts.
A death to the particulars.

Who I am passing over
from gnarled winter branches
to grow full again, flower,
welcome the challenge of becoming
a new season.

I am not yet ready to fall like the old oak
twice lightning struck and hurricane battered,
and merge with the leaves of my past years,
once and forever dead to the form.

But a little death I welcome.
A climax that opens my heart
to a new lover.
A striptease that leaves me blind
and bare, wide open to bud anew.
A melting into the Earth
before a strange new flower emerges:

red for my blood,
white for my bones,
bark black marrow
and mint green,
startled in the breeze
that is my breath.

Journey

A cave sparkles with crystal
colors, bedazzling passion
into possibilities. Each touch
a world, a journey, a life potential.

There: I give birth to a family.
Here: My children are words strung into necklace.

Each stone I touch, I pluck like fruit.
I bring to my lips, I swallow
light as it moves down my body, I digest
all possible wanderings.

I nourish with my body the seeds
and open my legs, open my legs,
push through new life,
push out potential, push out
butterflies and bring forth
bright faces that pour
out of pink crevices.

My sex gives life,
gives meaning.

Jewels fall from my core.
What I give precious, sacred
gift of Gaia.

Every moment I remember.
Every moment I forget.

Every moment I choose or do not choose,
I create.
I give birth
then wander among lilies,
intoxicated on scent and wine
and the chance to die.

I create through my body
something new.
I create and live
again.

Born out of the gush of the river
and into the ocean of still my time.

Life Eats

Life does not wait merely to die.
Life eats
cell by cell
mouthful by swallow.
Life tastes
microscopic beings on my skin;
life feasts on me.
I am a banquet,
an orgy of flavor,
and I feast in turn,
while balancing on a log,
crossing the river,
needing to nourish,
needing to be consumed.

There is something new coming,
coming as a tale,
a legend of a woman
who bore no fruit
yet gave birth to worlds.

Pregnant, she ate the vegetables,
the meat of creatures
to feed the being springing, sliding

out from between her legs,
birthing a dream:

a wild haired woman,
smoke eyes,
lean thighed,
small bellied and high in the trees.

It could be that her mouth
took root where babies emerge,
pushing into the world
a self that is healed.
Push into the world
the jewels of possibility.
Push into the world
her mind, her time,
her love, her awe,
a beast to ride on silken saddle.
No need to hide from the need
to be healed, whole,
happy, honored, unhindered,

a horse roaming the wide plain of all that exists.
Horse with one spiral horn.
Unicorn.

Lilies

Tigers stalk the sun.
Bees land on fangs,
lounge on the luxury of deep orange tongues,
drinking, drinking up life—
pure light nectar.
Hunger the same color
as being filled.
Orange, yellow,
warm wet
pollen slippers
and a bathrobe of dew.
Flowers hungry for little feet,
open wide and devour
the meat.

Forty Five

Changes come and bring a white
glaring indifference to how sunshine
ignites the window and eyes
unaccustomed to breathing light
shut before the enticement of living again.

There was a time when the greening
of the world brought wild dances
to these legs, and arms flames,
sinuous, reached toward my every desire.

I am not yet old but then I notice things.

Like how I can no longer eat what I want.
How bedtime calls long before midnight.
How strange drugs no longer court me.
How potential lovers grow grey beards
and fat tongues that fill my mouth.
How the fierce energy of children
sometimes irritates me.

I have always been a fan of change
and what it has brought to my growth.

But now, the change
feels like losing all the fresh leaves
of early summer in one fell swoop;
and winter dry wallowing, waiting
too long for the new cycle,
I look toward only a small dry cessation.

The end of it all.

Loving the Sky

Summer brings me back.
The tomb cannot claim me.
Not the endless maw of my end before me.
Not the edges of doubt that seep
and creep into the desire to believe
that I go on and on.

There is a chance that death is just that—
a finality.
An end of this fraction of time and space
I have taken as my pleasure.

But these are winter musings.
Today it is summer warm,
early morn' and already the air southern sultry
with the promise of sun feeding the garden.

It could be that like a child I simply accept
the moment as it is and not need a proof
beyond this certainty of my skin loving the sky.
But then again thoughts of cessation
came early for me. I was born old.

The laurel flowers wither to brown clots.

Summer dries away the wet vestiges of spring.
My skin crinkles and crimps
like hair let loose from braids.

Summer reminds me of plump flesh,
high rise breasts
and the juice of early peaches
I let run down my chin to drip, drop
on the sidewalk. Red life, falling in the groove
of my initials carved in the asphalt,
fills my name with the blood.

Here, I feast on such remnants.
Here where the summer courts remembrance—
This certainty.

Summer squash hardens,
new breasts of the young girls swell.
The sky ever blue romances
clouds that roil in the coming storm.

Loving.
My skin.

Sister Kisses

She kissed me in the dream,
full young lips soft and delicate.
Her tongue more knowing
than the old man of yesterday.
Her tongue quiet and tender,
moist against my tongue,
experienced. Not filling my mouth
as if to silence me
or dominate every orifice.
I do not now need
masculine possession.
Only the sweet shared solitude of sisters
who come together to sing the world into being.

Remembrance of Past Food

Pizza and crackers and sweet rolls
and bagels with cream cheese
sharp cheddar and apples
fresh baked bread with butter
and honey, and plums and peaches
and salad with croutons
croissants and eclairs
and spaghetti with meat balls
fried dough and candy canes
hot chocolate with marshmallow
baked beans and johnny cake
eggplant sub with hot peppers and
provolone, french fries
and Thai curry, samosas
and spicy burritos
nachos, potato chips
soda
salty peanuts
toast
omelet with spinach and swiss
lasagne
feta and red wine
thin mints and coffee
with sugar and thick, thick cream.

Wild Thing

You scream as you retreat to the wild woods.
For a week now you have laid claim to the land
I walk, the plants I gather for tea,
the fruit that drenches my lips,
the dandelion that I juice each morning.
Every night, we awaken to your harassment,
your cry that reveals you furious,
warning us away from this home.
Perhaps you have come because soon we will leave
to settle on another mountain. Perhaps
you have come to reclaim.
So far, I have yet to see you,
other than red devil eyes
glaring out from the center of some horrible
maw, sharp-toothed and in my worst fears, rabid
for my blood. But I have been reading too many vampire
books.
You are not some minion of Lestat come to make me
undead.
As my mother would say, you are more afraid of me.
I am not so wild, but I am much, much bigger than you.

Maiden

I will not know the joy of a swelling belly,
life meeting my life, my insides given over to a being
I would call my own, my own.

I will not know the ecstasy of being a woman
so completely. Of opening my body to its fullest
potential, of letting the flood pour out of me onto the
floor.

I will not know what it is to lose all modesty in the way
only a woman in labor must know. How all is given over
to the urge to push, push,
push out the love of my life into the world.

I will not know what it is to be so utterly in love that I
sacrifice all who I am for another. That I willingly give
my breasts over to another's claim.

I will not know the pleasure of seeing my lover loving the
being who my body nurtured and nurtures, of seeing in
his eyes such gratitude for my offering, my gift of life.

I will not know the full extent of what it is to be a
woman,

to open so wide the landscape falls into the rift,
and I become everything

I will not know.

First Fruit

Today I am Penelope,
floating in my own green boat.
My husband left in his red clipper
only to return when the tempest
sent him back into my arms.
I do not know how I got all the olives.
But here I am pressing, pressing
out oil as the boat rocks and rolls,
while my man in the hammock snores.
Now my arms come nowhere close to his
great bulges forged by sword and arrow.
But day after day of rendering oil
from armfuls of the tender fruit
will give a girl quite the biceps.
In my day there was no need
to go to the gym in lizard tight skin
like the girls of this age.
We women could not help but be strong.
Our sustenance demanded it.
One day you all will know.
Perhaps you will be pressing out your own oil,
or pounding grain into flour for your son's birthday cake,
wringing laundry by the river until your arms
pass ache into screech,

pulling weeds from your garden, digging a new outhouse,
or rowing your boat out into the wide sea,
wielding nets for fish to keep you through the long
winter.
Perhaps your man will be sleeping through the hot
afternoon
after a night out by moonlight hunting wild things.
You tip-toe to his side, bless his sun parched lips
with the sweet juice of the first ripe peach.

Today I Forgive

It is a release,
a letting go,
an offering to myself,
coming back to my
self.

No longer will I run miles
in my head, wondering
what went wrong.

Why I lost interest in your kisses
or how it was when that other man stopped loving me
when new flesh came around.

Today, I let it all be what it was
and wash it all in summer rain.

Tomorrow, or later today even,
I will watch it waver on the line.
See the sun dry the remnants
into mist that rises up to meet cloud.

The next storm and that old anger
will feed the garden.

I will eat the leaf and fruit
of my resurrection.

You will no longer be my obsession.
Who I most love to hate.

I will be a new person.

When I see you again
you will be surprised
when I touch your hand.

Thin Woman

She always wanted to be so thin,
remembers the teenage hunger
to look like a model,
remembers the disappointment.
No matter what she did
she would never be tall enough,
pretty enough,
thin enough.
She did not know how easy it could be.
Now in her forties, when eating
has become once again the struggle.
When gaining weight is the goal.
Unwelcome skinny birds come now
on the other end of hormonal rebellion.
Her body hungry on the wire
reels dizzy after a short flight.
She vomits not because she is afraid to be fat,
but because she cannot deal with
the consequences of eating
peanut butter, or sesame seeds,
or a piece of raw fruit.
This latest ordeal so tangible,
not like pining for a lover,
or her anger to never be alone.

This is her body.
This is her self trying to nourish
herself.
This is eating eggs
and meat after years of radical
vegan dogma.
This is cooking food again
after making the vow to eat
only food straight from the vine.
This is her body losing bulk,
her face becoming angular,
her breasts shrinking to the size of one palm.
When they talk about her
they say "oh, the skinny one."
She always wanted to be so thin.
And despite the suffering,
that makes her dinner plate
fashion model stingy,
she admits she is proud
of the way her thighs no longer touch,
the way the taut muscles in her belly
look against her underwear.
How she must find clothes still smaller
than those she wore at fifteen.
She knows it may not last,
in fact, hopes it does not.

She prays to the sky, the moon, the stars,
oh surely the stars will hear her wish
and grant it as the crickets dressed in powdered wigs
and french corsets laced tight sing her refrain.
Let her eat cake.
Let her eat cake.
Let her eat
CAKE!

Flowing Woman

Love how the rain comes to greet the morning,
and by afternoon the sun's hot rays dry the land.
The fickle mountain climate
suits the Goddess who waits by the stream,
admiring her own reflection,
in love with the trees, the clouds,
the faces that come to see themselves
in her flowing waters.
She never seems to hold on
long to one image of true love,
but embraces each new turn
as she moves down stream toward Sister Ocean.
The shifts and changes blend into pattern.
Every love she takes along the way
pours into one great cauldron,
a wine red broth that she drinks and drinks and drinks
before napping in the shade of poplar after the early rain.

The Fountain

For the healing there needs to be discipline.
The daily lemon drink.
The herbs that coat and love her from the inside.
The food that nourishes.
This preparing for the mighty crone to move in.
These years of saying goodbye to youth.

Even so, she feels young most of the time.
She knows a vitality in her bones
to bring her into white hair with lust still strong.
Somehow she knows she will always
fall in love with someone or something.
There will always be that something
she can drink or eat to feed her burgeoning immortality.

Today, tiny cobalt birds dance and scatter
like a shimmering, living fountain
before the wheels of her slow moving car.
Today, this road to awe reveals the way
to the great tree whose white blood
sprouts flowers inside her.

When she opens her mouth
she speaks in petals.

Gnome Down Under
Australia 2005

On the bluff, giant gnomes watch the sea.
Cheeks colour like the sand,
rough rock hewn from the spirit of the land,
and wild wiry hair sprouts from head and chin,
bush eyebrows poised for hearty laughter
exult in the midst of storm,
or ripple in the morning mist.

They speak of the ancient sunrise.
Assure me how they were once young.
Once upon a time, long, long ago,
they lived deep down,
down under the surface,
and made their way up
towards the call of a sensuous,
sultry, fickle and feisty woman.

Salty she was and is.
How she brought softness
to their skin, letting them watch
her dance, her undulations
toward them and away,
flicking them with her sweat,

the endless rhythmic tease.
How they hunger for the moments
of passion when she would rise
and wash over them in a fury
of delight, slashing and smashing
her body against their mouths,
bucking and rolling her juices
over their faces and hair,
making them hers
again and again and again,
sculpting lovers from stone

before leaving them quite alone.

Bear

Morning hungry for our scraps
and bits of last night's supper,
your snout rattles pots and razor edged cans,
scrounging for a taste of salmon, coconut milk,
sweet potato soup.
I awaken to the racket and see you.
Outside the window,
small, black and suddenly
disturbed by my presence.
You hesitate.
Look me in the eye,
You do not want to leave
the table of your feast.
I am okay with your staying.
I could make some compost tea
if you like, for a special treat.
After all, I am known in these parts
as a most gracious hostess.
You think about it a moment
before you lope uphill
and run away, run away.

Gift

I am here
Alive
Grateful
Changed
And changing
I accept
Life
I choose
Life
When I say I surrender
I do not mean
I give in
I will live this life
To the beautiful
Glorious end
That is not an end
I know this now
This is the gift
I have been given
I accept

End of Time

Woa Ha Hi

The time has come.
The time has come.

No more waiting for the clouds to descend,
fall upon the head of this body,
gather me up in creamy folds of plush:
a soft ride to heaven and my lips open for singing.

The time has come.

No need to wait for the perfect edge of verse
to attach to my magnet, to polarize
vision to the epitome of what it is to be blue
sky, or redder than blood, or golden yellow beech
leaf falling.

The time to open the bright foil gift wrapped package
sent straight from Antartica and filled
with the life and times of penguins.

Time to finally catch Santa as he falls
down brick to hearth, to offer him

sugar cookies from my small palm, to hear
the depth of his HO HO HO ringle rangle to my core.
The time has come to let loose the horses in the stall,
allow the soft brown mare to run again from plain
to plain into extraordinary speed, fed by joy,
by free at last, by cliff leaping fool love creating
pathways in the chaos of landscape, architecture
designed to fall away as I fall away,
as the life I know passes away in its time.

Here now the buildings gleam like glazed pots
set in the sun and decorated with the glittering,
shimmering, brilliant story of my life.

The time has come
to let the river flow, release the dams that have held
back the water's ecstatic gush to the sea, to let words,
song, dance, pantomime run free over the stones,
the dirt, against the bank that is my body, that holds
the torrent, the easy flow, the trickle.

Time
has come.

The calendar whizzes us all into breathtaking
sojourns into the lightning flash

change of all we ever knew
that we have waited for.
And now we welcome, heads thrown back,
pink, etheric yonis opening wide in the center
of our chests—receiving, receiving
Time, swallowing Time whole,
becoming one with Time,
and thus Time, no longer separate from us,
does not hold us to any yesterdays
or tomorrows.

Only Now.
Now has come.

Has always been here.
And now we see
And now we are
And now ever be

the ones we are waiting for.
The ones we are waiting for.
The One we are waiting for.
The One we are.

As each facet, you love and me,
rise to greet the end of time,

sing each our story,
melodies and harmonies entwined,
DNA of angels play harps and drums,
we dance around the fire to the call of our bodies,
our spirits rising with the smoke of song.

Yes, we reach to make love with the infinite black night.
Yes, we hold hands as we swirl and twirl
into endless upward spirals of delight.
Yes.
Yes.
Yes
We Howl
to the ever holy bliss beat
of now love
now life,
now a soft blown kiss
now carried by the wind to stars
now dance
now dream
now live this life moment to moment
to blessed moment
as creators, as one with source
as healers moving beyond the illusion
of you as separate from me
as us as separate from them

we *come together, right now,*
right now,

Unity.

Cancer

What it is like to be the you
swimming inside the me—
diagnosis
that suddenly seeks
to define
a world patterned
by stars shining
against midnight blue,
lovers lounging on scarlet sheets,
a body moving to the dance
of a life made my own way?
Are you as frightened as I am to die?
Often I awake at three am
with terror drenching the blankets.
So the doctor opened my belly,
took out my potential to give life
and the danger of you spreading
yourself like thin black jam
sits on my head, waiting for the tea
and biscuits once promised.
I dare not serve.
Perhaps if I am a nice enough hostess,
you will go away before you wear out
your welcome.

Perhaps if I give you a sweet or two,
acknowledge your hunger,
then you will realize there is no need
to eat all of me.
I am very giving.
Very compassionate.
But I will not let you eat me out
of house and home.
I know you need love.
We all do.
How about letting the white rabbit
nibble on your edges,
ingest you and allow you to heal
and be a part of the healthy
me that lives?
That is the answer.
You and I are dancing
a dance of dark and light.
I hear what you show me.
I understand what must change in me.
Your change will be what you most long for,
even if you do not know it yet.
Cells of mine, turned dark crystal,
reach for your light sisters;
they long to embrace you,
kiss you,

hold you through the night
until your transformation
brings complete healing.
My body will thrive then.
Come on. We can do it.
Together.
Feel ourselves be swallowed
by the cloud of light.
Feel the malignancy become love.
I will always honor you, your darkness,
and bless your ability to become white
as the sunrise,
bright, a healer from within.
Cell by cell.
Hold my hand.
Okay, ready?
Let's jump into God.

Circles

I live in a circle
surrounded by a circle
my family a circle
circle joining circle
my northern circle
my southern circle
connect through the circle
I make with my lover
most precious circle of all
I have no child to make that circle
but maybe step-grandchildren will come
the circle of healers
the circle of artists
the circle of spiritual seekers
the circle of my natal family
the circle of old lovers now dissipates
the circle of new loves emerges
the circle of old friends reconnecting
the circle of the planet
circles within circles
with no beginning
and never ending

Shiva Says

Every person you know will one day die.
Years from now or tomorrow
we pass from living, breathing being
into the infinity of another reality.
It is a mystery. The greatest of all.
As mysterious as life
and consciousness.
As all encompassing as love.

Aronia Nero

On the day of our hand fasting
we planted Aronia Nero
at the far edge of the garden.
November blew its first frosty breath.
Our fingers reached for the earth to fill
the hole and hold the roots firm
and mold the already formed buds
in position to pray to the sky.
Red leaves like harlot hair
brushed our cheeks as we watered
our future food with joy.
One day soon there will be berries to feed
the cells and make our eyes shine
even brighter.
One day there will be dry wine to offer to our favorite
god.
One day we will dry and otherwise preserve
the fruit that burgeons from this now small sapling.
Until then, we offer thanks and prayers,
visions of green leaves
and deep blue fruit,
our own dark waste to feed you
as you feed us,
as we together feed mother earth

with leaf, with flesh,
with hands held together by cord.
In spring we will lay naked with Aronia,
let white flowers caress us,
plant our own bright seed
and grow, grow, grow.

Womb Space

Empty.

Oh, beautiful muscle taken away.
Oh, world shaped ovaries gone.
Fallopian tubes, cervix
all cut out by the surgeon's hand.

I allowed this to happen.
It was fear, perhaps even necessary
to save my life.

Oh, beautiful belly sewn up now
crooked. I do not much mind the scar,
but the dimples from the uneven
stitches make me cry:
two extra puckers in the once
smooth skin. Two extra frowns
or smiles if I stand on my head.

Oh, I am a woman after all,
even if I am also human
seducing mortality for more time.

Without my once perfect belly,

those sacred organs,
without the blood flow
(oh, never again to bleed on Mother Earth!)
without the tidal rhythm of moon light
surging in my womb space,
now, there is just space.

A cavern emptied of stones.
A house swept of furniture.
A forest bereft of trees.

No longer can I say "my womb."
Oh, but I can talk about the space left.

How the energy of those organs
lingers in a bath of orange light.
How I, maiden tantrika, reconnect
the energetic dots
with an orange crayon.

Orange sunset.
Orange tiger lily.
Orange sweet potato, carrot soup.
Orange pumpkin slow roasted over coals.
Beta carotene orange for cellular surprise.

My belly swells in the orange light of dawn.
I give birth now to citrus trees and bloom white flowers.
I am woman with breasts and belly and clitoris
pert pink and sensitive.

When I come the spaces fill
with much more than a memory of flesh.

Oh, I am filled with the child of my love for living
as woman, as energetic diva, as lover,
as taster, as keeper of the many shades of sensual;

emotional, sexy bright and sun kissed orange space,
womb space, oh palace, oh ripe as midnight;

ancient One birthing the dawn.

Queen

In thirteen moons,
according to body lore,
I be Crone.
As this was brought on
not by my natural cycle,
but the cutting away of my blood right,
I feel more Queen,

Amazon
coming into her power,
scepter dazzling,
bow and arrow poised,
wearing a crown
of rhododendron branches
and chickadee.

The carpet of leaves
cushions my bare feet.
My cape woven of bamboo
and moonlight,
dyed poke berry purple.

I walk the land
while doors open for me.

I walk on through
to greet bear, raccoon,
skunk and crow.

Hawk circles three times overhead
at my coronation.
The young women squeal and sing,
inspired by my example.

I am not here to rule
but to offer myself
as helper to you.

Just hold my hand.
Brush your lips over my fingers.
Kiss my silver ring.
Rise from your knees.

Hug me, Sister!
Hug me, Brother!

Let us walk together to the altar
and receive there
the story of our lives.

One Ring
For Frodo

There is a ring.
It is silver, etched
leaves dance across
the band.
It is placed on my finger
by my self for better or even better,
for challenge and more challenge,
for love of who I am
and the glitter of spirit dust
I sprinkle as I walk the world.
When I wear this ring
I do not disappear,
but come to you clearer
with eyes unveiled and luminous.
As you watch, you could swear my ears grow pointed.

The journey through darkness
drones hunger laden, tiring, cold and wet
with no sign of ending,
the climb up the mountain,
the steep stairs, the stalker Gollum,
the leviathan spider
who dresses me in white silk,

invites me to a late night dinner.
All the rings of gold melt in the fires of doom,
the reptilian mind slinks back to its place.
I find I am naked, lava burns and my temperature
rises, rises, burning breath roasts me
to the perfect tenderness.

After all the gold madness passes,
it is silver, silver that calls to me.

Silver crown
silver necklace
silver bracelet
silver mail
silver pin
silver ring etched with leaves,

made in Rivendell
by elves.

Disciple

As disciple of Her
I learn to breathe.
My discipline to rise each morning
and breakfast on tree breath.

As disciple of Her
I learn to do.
My discipline to greet the noon
with tools and sweat.

As disciple of Her
I learn to flow.
My discipline to approach twilight
wet with creek water.

As disciple of Her
I learn to stay.
My discipline to sit at midnight
as still as stone.

As disciple of Her
I learn to be.
My discipline to dance in the center
and radiate sunlight from my heart.

Different

for Paulo Coelho and the Witch

Dedicated to difference
I walk the land barefoot,
let earth energy surge upward,
let Divine Feminine love change me
to who I was born to be.

Blessed outsider,
I walk the streets smiling,
notice the squirrels nibbling fries,
the pigeons pecking popcorn
from the curbside.

At school they called me different.
My owl eyes that saw everything
too invasive, too knowing.
"Look how she stares!"
Beautiful girls in college
pierced me with frowns
for my admiration.
Afraid I might kiss them
or that I am staring at an ugliness
only they cannot appreciate.

So true.

I see the horror with the beauty.

Side by side.

I hold these together in my whole.

I see them in you and love you for it.

Human is this:

the ability to hold everything

and at the same time

nothing at all.

Goddess Mountain
for Mama Tiana

Soon, I journey into snow.
From one mountain range to another,
I travel to that other home
where I was born.
The peaks are smaller there.
The forest not so wild.
But it is where it all began.

So I return to the source.
Healing awaits in the cold blasts
of a Nor'Easter.
Healing awaits in the warm smiles
of family who wish me love and long life.

I will live this time.
Live to be an old woman.
Live to create this new home
in the southern realm.
Live to take on the accent
of the Appalachian mountain folk.

Live to build my house with these hands.
Live to feed my garden with this heart.

Live to give my new community all who I am.
Live to return to that other home
again and again and again.

Clean Water

I rise before dawn each day.
My body adjusts to the changes
and sleep no longer easy.
I gaze at the bottles of supplements,
tinctures, healing herbs.
Some mornings I feel overwhelmed.
But gratitude
comes to have the knowledge of how to heal
passed on by the courage and love of so many.
I will not flood my body with chemicals
or irradiate my cells.
I will not piss poison into the water supply.
I am Earth Keeper and envisioning a pure Earth
is my job. I cannot add to the pain.
My life is worth more than that.
I am here to help heal my Mother
through my own transmutation,
my own healing of the dis ease.
My body her body.
I accept the path of the healer.
I accept my path to life
and green fields, blue skies,
clean water.
I accept my path to love.

I will not do anything to heal.
Only that which serves
myself
and all my relations.

Shaman

In her eye
I saw my healing
complete.
"No cancer"
she told me.
No cancer.
I knew then the truth.
How as a young girl
I fell into water and hurt my ovary.
How I have been nervous
and worried ever since,
afraid and feeling unsafe
in the world.
Now at 45
I am dealing.
Now at 45
after a lifetime of carrying the fear,
I am healed.
Fear gone.
Malignancy gone.
My body pure again.
I want to share it with everyone.
Let everyone know how easy it was.
How God and Angels came to help me.

How these twin shamans came,
put their hands on my belly,
my head, my grief
and blessed me
with long life.
Gracias.

Creek

Calls me into
cold cellophane
cells crackle
crimp back skin
collage with stone.
Cotillion of ions
crest breasts
caught in waterfall,
calves float
crisp as apples
crunch against pebbles
cry of the white pine
catalyst heals even
cancer, even
cynicism.
Come into the
cold, cold November.
Cedar bark kisses
comfort blue
corpse of ovaries
culled from blood,
crimson
clotted forest
cemetery

covered by oak leaves
crust of another dawn.

Sweet Miss Holly

Gifted by gratitude
I call and give thanks.
Sweet Miss Holly
surprised, so often not thanked
for her kindness.
Glad I am to be the bright
voice giving in return
for her giving me what I need.
In this instance,
disability cash to help fund healing
visits to Spirit Tribe,
naturopaths,
sessions with shamans,
food for my Aphrodite body.
Sweet Miss Holly, Social Worker
to the Stars.

Teachers

The trees
shorn of shimmer,
reach toward light.

The trees show my own branches
how to put on cloud,
show me how to wear the sky.
Pine needles sewn into sky skirt
wrap around bark calves,
layers of death around thick
mountain, root solid,
toes entwined in winter earth.

The trees teach.

We are firm on the mother ellipse.
And we sway in the wind.

I understand.

All the best dancers
know how to jump
without fear into air
and land solid

as trees,
as stones,
or mountains,

on the sacred
ground.

SOPHIA

Wise Momma's mirrored skirt flirts with scintillating.
Sure pond and lotus reflect the frown, the joy right back
at you.

Her shirt brown, scented with myriad mugwort and
myrrh,
grounded in earth, dirt, an early garden.

Light sparkles from her fingernails,
flesh colored iris shimmies up
your bare naked thigh

to get you high.

Homo Luminous

Winter has been kind to recent southern skin.
January comes and we walk still on earth.
Hades waits; the earth
still vital, not yet fully frozen.
Vague fears that his bride might
get it in my head to find my mother
sooner than promised, dropping
seeds from my tongue as I wander off
to dig my way to the surface and emerge
green and slender and vulnerable.
Even he helpless to bring on the bitter
wind, the cold that pierces bone.

But it comes.
Just yesterday at the beach, I felt it.
The lovemaking between river and ocean
was waves bucking hips.
Slow grind against crest of foam
and moans rising with each crash
and crumble back from sand.

A sudden shift to arctic threnody,
howls over my dreams.
Trees wail when branches fall.

The cold comes to claim
again my form.

Defiant, my body pink and vital palms life orange,
I climb my way to the surface,
fingernails dig into soil,
teeth bite through roots,
crown pushes, pushes
through the ever widening opening
that pulses to give birth to spring.

Somewhere in the middle of this climb
the snow tumbles over the land.
I halt, caught in the middle.
Not with my lover below.
Not with my mother above.
Alone in the tunnel.
Curled up and black as a beetle.
As it must be to grow me.

Between parachutes and landings,
I await a beginning
to rival all beginnings.
I wait for
the end of time

so I can breathe again
with new lips,
speak again with a new mouth,
love again with new arms
and hands and fingernails
holding mere fragments
of my journey, my history,
the long story that propels me into the light,
the light, the Light.

What I Can Eat

This potato is sweet,
flesh yellow and firm, or bright orange
vitamin A banquet,
delicious roasted with cinnamon
and Himalayan sea salt,
delicious in soup
with carrots and pepper
and celery,
delicious steamed with salt
and mashed into no fat, gluten free muffins.

Some say yam.
Yes, Ma'am.
Yam.

In the Andes,
a strong spirit people have lived on just about
only the meaty sweet delightful yam
for aeons.

Life can be that simple.

Breakfast: yam mash with honey.
Lunch: yam soup with ginger

Supper: roasted yam cinnamon surprise.
Guess what's for dinner tonight
and tomorrow and the next day?
The sweetly delectable, irresistible,
hearty, whole and yes, horny

Yam!

Faery Land

I have learned not to ask for patience.
Now what I need is a miracle.
A sudden change of weather
to fly in on the wind.
An overnight evolution,
waking to a body made for dancing,
making love, working with the land.
A transformation to come and lift
my love to the next level of consciousness,
where all is just part of the whole thing
that is happening. Where each level of understanding
can be realized fully in me and then more to come.
I am not looking for a guru or god to perform
the grand illusion of my change.
I am not looking to be right about anything.
I am just creating here and now,
with words and what I do,
with my smile and my delight.
With I choose life.
With I choose growth.
With I choose healing.
With I acknowledge that I am a part of the swirling,

whirling, reds riding yellow sunlight,
orange hitching the green bus,
blue so grateful to find itself violets
blooming and the edges of petals
dipped in the white juice of dandelion.

In this moment
everything new.

One, two, three⋯
Now.

.

4422353R00046

Made in the USA
San Bernardino, CA
21 September 2013